This journal belongs to :

_____

Notes

Notes

Her Goals

Month: _____

This month's goals:

_____
_____
_____
_____
_____

Why I want it:	Reward:

Action steps:

_____
_____
_____
_____

Deadline:

_____
_____
_____
_____

Notes:

_____
_____
_____

Notes

Work hard for your dreams because no one else will.

Her Goals

Month: _____

This month's goals:

_____
_____
_____
_____
_____

Why I want it:	Reward:
_____	
_____	
_____	
_____	

Action steps: Deadline:

_____   _____

_____   _____

_____   _____

_____   _____

Notes:

_____
_____
_____

Notes

Notes

Set goals that make you want to jump out of bed in the morning.

Her Goals

Month: _____

This month's goals:
_____
_____
_____
_____
_____

Why I want it:	Reward:

Action steps: Deadline:
_____   _____
_____   _____
_____   _____
_____   _____

Notes:
_____
_____
_____

Notes

Notes

Notes

Set goals.
Work hard.
Stay out the way.

Her Goals

Month: _____

This month's goals:

_____
_____
_____
_____
_____

Why I want it:	Reward:

Action steps: Deadline:

_____   _____

_____   _____

_____   _____

_____   _____

Notes:

_____
_____
_____

Notes

Notes

Have goals so big, you get uncomfortable telling the small minded.

Her Goals

Month: _____

This month's goals:

_____
_____
_____
_____
_____

Why I want it:	Reward:

Action steps: Deadline:

_____   _____
_____   _____
_____   _____
_____   _____

Notes:

_____
_____
_____

Notes

Notes

Do something today that will bring you one step closer to those goals.

Her Goals

Month: _____

This month's goals:

_____
_____
_____
_____
_____

Why I want it:	Reward:

Action steps: Deadline:

_____   _____

_____   _____

_____   _____

_____   _____

Notes:

_____
_____
_____

Notes

Notes

If there's one thing I'm willing to bet on.. it's myself

Her Goals

Month: _____

This month's goals:

_____
_____
_____
_____
_____
_____

Why I want it:	Reward:

Action steps: Deadline:

_____   _____

_____   _____

_____   _____

_____   _____

Notes:

_____
_____
_____

Notes

Notes

Wake up, say your prayers, Slay those goals.

Her Goals

Month: _____

This month's goals:

_____
_____
_____
_____
_____

Why I want it:	Reward:

Action steps:

_____
_____
_____
_____

Deadline:

_____
_____
_____
_____

Notes:

_____
_____
_____

Notes

Notes

Keep showing up for those goals, girl.

Her Goals

Month: _____

This month's goals:

_____
_____
_____
_____
_____

Why I want it:	Reward:

Action steps:

_____

_____

_____

_____

Deadline:

_____

_____

_____

_____

Notes:

_____
_____
_____

Notes

Notes

She's motivated by the fear of being average.

Notes

She's motivated by the fear of being average.

Her Goals

Month: _____

This month's goals:
_____
_____
_____
_____
_____

Why I want it:	Reward:

Action steps: Deadline:

_____   _____
_____   _____
_____   _____
_____   _____

Notes:
_____
_____
_____

Notes

Notes

Work for it more than you hope for it.

Her Goals

Month: _____

This month's goals:

_____
_____
_____
_____
_____

Why I want it:	Reward:

Action steps: Deadline:

_____   _____
_____   _____
_____   _____
_____   _____
_____   _____

Notes:

_____
_____
_____

Notes

Notes

Her Goals

Month: _____

This month's goals:

_____
_____
_____
_____
_____

Why I want it:	Reward:

Action steps: Deadline:

_____   _____
_____   _____
_____   _____
_____   _____

Notes:

_____
_____
_____

Notes

Notes

Notes

Notes

Notes

Notes

Notes

Notes

Notes

Notes

Notes

Notes

Notes

Notes

Notes

Notes

Notes

Notes

Notes

Notes

Notes

Notes

Notes

Notes

Notes

Notes

Notes

Notes

Notes

Notes

Notes

Notes

Notes

Notes

Notes

Notes

Notes

Notes

Notes

Notes

Notes

Notes

Notes

Notes

Notes

Notes

Notes

Notes

Notes

Notes

Notes

Notes

Notes